BREAKING THE POWER OF UNKNOWN CURSE

Pastor Elijah Oluwole

Breaking The Power Of Unknown Curse.

Published by
Beeni Global Resources
381, Borno Way,
Yaba,
Lagos, Nigeria.
PO Box 3405, Somolu,
Lagos, Nigeria.
Tel: +2348033225953/+2349096991619
beeniglobalresources@gmail.com

ISBN: 978-978-942-915-8

Pastor Elijah Oluwole asserts the moral right to be identified as the author of this work under the copyright laws.

Introduction

Let us look at Deuteronomy 28:45-47:

Moreover all these curses shall come upon thee and shall purse thee and overtake thee, till thou be destroyed. Because thou hearkened not unto the voice of the Lord thy God to keep his commandments and his statutes which he commanded thee. And they shall be upon thee for a sign and a wonder and upon thy seed forever, because thou servest not the Lord thy God with joyfulness and with gladness of heart, for the abundance of all things.

A lot of people are suffering and are in bondage. A sister asked me a question sometime ago. She said, "Pastor, are there still genuine pastors in Nigeria?" I was shocked when another brother brought up the same question.

In the bible passage above, serving people is not serving God. It says because thou hearkened not unto the voice of the Lord thy God, they are rebellious. What did they serve, they served other gods .Because they served other gods, God placed a curse on them. He said because they served not the Lord their God, they are serving other gods which is not the true God so curse shall be on them and it shall be upon their seeds.

I encountered a man of God from Cameroun. He started by speaking big vocabulary but I told him that he if he would speak his native language that he will be alright. You know to forcefully speak through your nose is also a big calamity.

After he narrated his ordeal, I told him what his problem was. I showed him portions in the bible and prayed with him

Brethren, there are some prayers that cannot be effective until you pray them in your native language.

God created your mouth to talk so why turn your smelling junction to speaking junction. Your nose is to be used for smelling and breathing and not for speaking.

I pray that God opens your eyes to understand the message in this book in Jesus name

Unknown curse is real

As we go deeper into this book, you will understand that there are some deadly surnames .Your surname came from your parents, particularly your paternal line, so who and what your first father served played a purpose in the kind of surname they chose. If he served an idol and though the idol was already removed before we arrived we should know that it is still in the spirit; most idols are removed on the surface but not from the spirit.

 They are no more on the surface because they will look too old. Now your fathers did not serve God, they served idols and because they served idols there is a curse on them that is what the bible says. And that curse automatically cleaved to you because you are from the same bloodline with them. The curse is not in your spirit, it is in your blood and the funniest thing is that your blood is not born again. That power of unknown curse is working in your blood against you, that is why there is a mysterious problem you cannot handle and your Pastor cannot handle it also.

Some Pastor would tell you " for this your problem to vanish, you need to make a very solid sacrifice and offering and as the Lord has blessed you so would your offering be."

Let me make a pure correction here: paying tithes regularly, offering sacrifice or libations cannot break your curse. What will break your curse is to know the truth about your curse and to pray for God's mercy to break it because there are a lot of errors while trying to break a curse.

This curse you are talking about is not the one you put upon yourself. If you curse yourself, it will be known that you cursed yourself. If your parents cursed you, you will know that your parents cursed you. If your friend cursed you, you will know that your friend cursed you but if a curse is on your great grandfather, how would you know. If a curse is on your father, how would you know? If a curse is on your village and on all the sons and daughters that were born in that village, how would you know?

A typical example of an unknown curse is when you go to some villages; they make a calamitous pronouncement on any son and daughter of the soil that refuses to serve the idol/deity. Many of us were not there when they were making those pronouncements. That curse shall continue to be transferred from generation to generation until somebody appears to stand against it and break it.

Many people are faced by witches and wizards. The reason why they have power over you is because they know there is a curse in your bloodline. When they go to your bloodline to ask what kills the people in your family, they will be able to hinge on the lineage curse in your bloodline to wreak havoc.

God said that this curse shall come upon you because you disobeyed. You see there is a danger in disobeying God and there is also danger in breaking His law. If you do not stand up and fight this curse, it will finally conquer you and pass over to your children.

Biblical case

Gehazi was a servant of Elisha, he did something very bad in the ministry and Elisha said that the leprosy of Namaan shall leave him alone and cleave unto him. The man of God will have kept his mouth like that and let the man suffer for what he has done but you know that is not how a curse works..

Some will put it this way: The iniquity of the father shall not be on the son, the son shall bear his iniquity and the father shall bear his own iniquity. Do those preachers really understand the bible? Are we talking about iniquity? Does that place have anything to do with iniquity? The bible did not say that the curse of the father will not come upon the son; it says iniquity which is sin. If the son repents, his sin will be forgiven, the father will be judged for his sin but the curse that follows that father, bible did not say it will not come upon the son.

It says Namaan listen to this, **"Leprosy shall be on you and it shall be on your seed"** and it was so.

Even the day of Jesus, the Jews were asked who should be released to them and they said, "Give us Barabbas, away with Jesus". Then Pilate said, "I wash my hands clean", and they said, "Let the curse be upon us and upon our children".

That curse is still fighting the Jews till today and they know it. You see that is why you must pray, that thing that is happening in your life is not just a mere accident neither is it a mere coincidence. Some will say this thing happening to me is coincidental.

My friend those demons will say it is you who is saying it is coincidental and the y will just laugh and say we are having a good time while you are speaking grammar.

True life story.

A young man was working in an oil company where they gave him a good car and a good house and his children were going to a good private school.

One day the wife walked up to me and shared some happenings in their family, later she brought her husband. After hearing them out, I told the husband that he should break the curse upon his head.

The man said "Pastor, I do not believe in that shit, I got nothing to do with it".

He told me that he has nothing to do with that fucking African bullshit(pardon my French).I told him that demon does not understand grammar and I finally told him, "Sir, the day they will come for you, your pastor will not be able to deliver you ,so you better deliver yourself now because a curse is following you".

He just took his wife and walked away.

A year later they came back. They had thrown him out of that oil company like a nobody and collected his accommodation and his cars and he was literarily turning to a beggar. All his children were withdrawn from private school and sent to public school. His wife that was a full time housewife started learning tailoring.

Please look for the source of your problem, things do not just happen, something must have caused it.

What makes you go to the mountain and pray and fast and still come back and remain the way you are is unknown curse. What makes a pastor to pray with you always and you remain the same is also unknown curse, it is cleaving to you.

How do you come out of it?

There is no way you can come out of it without prayers. It is the power of prayers but people do not want to pray, it's the truth.
Steps to follow;

Repent from your sins because the curse came in the first place due to sin. It said because you did not serve the Lord your God, you did not obey his statutes, so start obeying God. Repent from your sins; tell the Lord that you are sorry.

Confess your sins to him. Many people today do not want to come out of their sins; they will tell you they are born again, what kind of being born again is still committing adultery, fornication, doing evil yet you call yourself a born again Christian. Truly repent from your sins, repent genuinely and also repent whole heartedly. Confess your sins.

Open your heart and surrender your life to the Lord Jesus. Jesus died that you might be saved; he rose again on the third day that you might be saved.

Accept Jesus as your Lord and Saviour. Let no man deceive you and you do not go on deceiving yourself, that is why the yoke of an unknown curse will not be broken from your head. Brother Paul said something, he said, "We then as workers together with him beseech ye also that we receive not the grace of God in vain". Don't be under vain grace, let the grace be real in your life.

I was talking to a young man and a lady that were courting recently and I said ,"Are you born again?" and the man answered "yes" and I turned to the lady and repeated the same question, she replied in the affirmative. I asked them how many years they have been born again and the guy told me five years. I then asked them how many times they have had sex in the courtship and they said three times. I then asked them so they have had sex three times in their courtship and they claim they are still born again, and they said "Pastor yes, that is the type of born again we have nowadays."

If you ask some housewives whether they are born again, they will tell you that they are born again. If you ask them how many toy boys (young boyfriends) they have, they will tell you they have only one, yet, they are born again. Curse cannot be broken from your head like that because you are still living in sin. If you say you are under grace then the grace upon you is in vain, first of all repent from your sin and come out of sin outrightly.

A lady came to me to pray for her and I asked her whether she has surrendered her live to Christ, she said yes, and when i repeatedly ask the same question she still said yes.

I said no problem, let us pray. I said Father, break this curse and you spirit controlling the curse come out. The demon did not come out and said pastor, you asked this lady a question whether she is born again and she said yes. You equally asked her if she is living in sin and she said no, I'm here to tell you I'm not coming out because she is living in sin. I asked the demon what kind of sin and it told me that she had committed many abortions.

I turned to the lady and asked her why she did not confess her sin in the first place but she could not say anything reasonable.

Sin will not allow God to set you free, God wants to set you free but the demons will not go because of sin.

If you want to be a Christian, be a genuine Christian, repent from your sin, surrender your life to Jesus Christ and let Him be your Lord and Saviour, then He will save you and set you free so that when we command the yoke to be broken the curse will be broken and you will begin to enjoy your life.

Wrong ways to go about deliverance from an unknown Curse.

God said freely you receive and freely shall you give. Some people think they have carry bags of money to pastors before they can be delivered and problems will be solved and that is why some so called men of God are making merchandise out of you. Many people think Pastors that do not collect money from people to pray for them or conduct deliverance do not know what I'm doing.

Many do not want to repent from their sins and still want to enjoy the goodness of God. It is due to sin that your ancestors brought curse upon you, you should repent from that sin so that the curse can be broken off you.

Let me put it bluntly, anyone that billed you in the name of carrying out deliverance for you is a big scam. After you have been fleeced of your finance, the problem will persist, in fact, they just introduced you into a greater bondage. That is not what can deliver you.

Hear the truth of freedom, repent from your sin,

Your case is a very serious case and the spirit says, I must see your nakedness three times so that the ancestral curse can be broken. You too will open your

I do not know maybe you have suffered from that curse, hear the truth, listen to the truth and obey the truth. Repent from your sins, surrender your life to Jesus, let Him be your Lord and saviour, and then start obeying God.

The effectual fervent prayer of a righteous man availeth much.

Pray and the power of prayer will break the curse.

Finally the minister of God will pray for you and the curse will be broken. If you find your little children misbehaving do not beat or curse them, bring them to God. Please do not let anyone beat your child in the name of deliverance from familiar spirits. Children are to be taken care of, they are to be loved. Jesus said, *"Let the children come unto me for theirs the kingdom of God "* . Do not beat that innocent child; he/she does not know how they were possessed.

Is it not your grandparents that made the covenant? Don't ask a child to fast for three days or seven days. Why and for what reason should a child go on dry fast, because you want to deliver her from familiar spirits?

Some people will say that if a child cries at night, that the child belongs to occult, you cut the child and put pepper on his/her body that is another bondage that is false teaching.

If a child is hungry or wets his pants, the only way he can pass the message is by crying. If you understand his language and feed him, change his nappy and rock him up and down, he will keep quiet.

When your child cries in the night, it could be that some people are tormenting him. Pray for the child; do not call him a witch. You can take the child to a good church to be prayed for and the evil spirit will go away.

By trying to break ancestral curses on their children, many parents have put their children into problem with some funny characters. They allow those people to demonize their children. They will tell you not to allow the child eat with you, don't let the child use the same cup with you.

Even if the child has HIV, will you kill him?

Some maltreat those children, push them aside and lock them up. Go to some places; they lock children in rooms even in cages saying they are witches and they should not come out and they will be feeding them with food of affliction, saying they must confess, that is another bondage.

Do not let anybody do that to your child, they will tell

you they want to deliver them by force, you don't deliver people by force. All you need to do is pray and let the minister of God who has the spirit of Christ pray with the child.

Personal experience

I was ministering in a place and when I started praying with them, a little boy of about four years old walked up to me and held my hand and asked that we go out to have a chat.

When we got there I asked, "What do you want? " The little boy said, "You see there is a power inside you, that power is big and there is a power inside me but that power is bad, I want the power inside me to go out so that the one inside you can come in, so how do we do it, let us do it here".

I said "that it was very simple", but he said," I am a wizard, a very big wizard but I don't like it again, I want the power inside you".

I told him that it was easy and that we should pray: In the name of Jesus, Father, forgive me, I confess, I reject it, wash me with the blood. Jesus, come into my heart, Amen. I renounce it in Jesus name. Satan I hate you, go away (He repeated all after me). Then I told him to close his eyes and I prayed, you wizard jump out in Jesus name, Holy Ghost enter.

I told him to open his eyes and the boy opened his eyes and said "the thing has gone." You see what is inside you is now inside me. That was how the boy was delivered, no cane, no beating, no shouting

A young boy has leukemia (cancer of the blood). The family spent so much to treat him. We were invited to the hospital to see him. When we got there, the boy was like "oh pastor welcome" and we were laughing and we told him that Jesus loves him. I asked him whether he wanted Jesus and he said yes, I receive him.

I told him to say Jesus, heal me and he repeated. I now said you leukemia jump out in the name of Jesus and be healed and the boy jumped up immediately. When medical experts c came back the next day, they carried out all sorts of medical tests on the boy but did not see any sign of leukemia and the boy was discharged instantly.

I do not know the curse on you but it shall be broken in Jesus name.

Prayer of confession.

Dear Father, have mercy upon me. I confess my sin unto you. Father, forgive me. I believe in the blood of Jesus. Father wash me now, cleanse now from all my sins with blood of Jesus. Lord Jesus I believe with all my heart that you are the son of God

You died for my sin. You were buried and rose again on the third day. Lord Jesus, I receive you today as my Saviour and my Master. Come into my heart; give me the power to sin no more. Lord Jesus, write my name in the book of life, Amen.

Prayers.

- In the name of Jesus, God of all mercy, arise and have mercy upon my life.
- Every generation and foundation pollution in my life, blood of Jesus wipe them away.
- In the name of Jesus, generational curse in my life, hear the word of the Lord, break.
- In the name of Jesus, power of unknown curses, troubling my life, your time is up, die
- You power of an unknown curse that attacked my grandfather, that attacked my father, that attacked my grandmother, that attacked my mother, you power of unknown curse that is attacking them in my village, hear the word of the Lord, I am no more your candidate therefore die in the name of Jesus.
- In the name of Jesus, power of an unknown curse that conquered my great grandfather, that conquered my father, that conquered my great grandmother, that conquered my mother, that conquered them in my village, that conquered them in my father's house that is working in my life, I am not your candidate, my children are not your candidate, my husband is not your candidate, my wife is not your candidate, therefore die.

- In the name of Jesus, power that controls curses in my father's house, in my village, hear the word of the Lord appear.
- In the name of Jesus, power that control unknown curses in my life, hear the word of the Lord, appear.
- Now that you have appeared, you have no more power over my life, you have no more power over my children, you have no more power over my husband, you have no more power over my wife, you have no more power over my health, you have no more power over my finances, therefore die in the name of Jesus.
- In the name of Jesus, arrow of unknown curses in my life, in the life of my husband, in the life of my wife, in the life of my children, hear the word of the Lord, die
- Anointing that breaks every yoke, arise and break my yoke in Jesus name.
- God of all power, pour your power upon my life and bring me out of the bondage of generational curse.
- In the name of Jesus, the generational curse that said I must suffer the same way my forebears suffer release me and die in the name of Jesus.
- In the name of Jesus, the generational curses that conquered my ancestors with strange afflictions and disease that is afflicting my life with the same symptoms, hear the word of the

Lord, I am not your candidate so therefore, die in the name of Jesus.

- Power of unknown generational curses that caged my glory not to manifest, break in the name of Jesus.
- Anointing that will make me to recover and enjoy what my forebears did not enjoy, arise from the presence of God and envelope me in the name of Jesus.
- I decree in the name of Jesus from today, the blessing of God in my life shall supersede generational curse.
- From today, I stand and remain on the mountain of blessings in the name of Jesus.
- I decree my closed doors from ancient times; hear the word of the Lord, open in the name of Jesus.
- By the anointing and power of the God of Elijah, I overrun and overtake those who have gone ahead of me in the journey of destiny in the name of Jesus.
- I decree, my testimony shall be loud and sound now in Jesus name.
- I decree and declare in the name of Jesus, I am blessed and I am favored. (21 times).
- I decree and declare, oh Lord, heal me and I shall be healed .(21 times).